Smart Ads

Ant Millionblair

Copyright © 2020 by Ant Millionblair

Table Of Contents

Dedications 1

Introduction 2

Chapter 1: Smart vs. Ignorant Advertising 7

Chapter 2: Testing Your Smart Advertising 10

Chapter 3: How Does Smart Advertising Work? 13

Chapter 4: Headlines 16

Chapter 5: The Psychology of Advertising That Wins 18

Chapter 6: Competitive Advantage 20

Chapter 7: Benefits Versus Features 22

Chapter 8: How to Make Offers Irresistible 24

Essential Headline and Attention Grabber Companion 29

Greatest Headlines Ever Written 30

Attention Grabber Words 38

Quotes from the GOATS 41

Leo Burnett 41

Fairfax M. Cone 45

Claude C. Hopkins 49

Maxwell Sackheim 53

John Caples 65

Dedications

This book was a long time coming. Twenty-three years to be exact. I went to a Peter Lowe seminar back when those were all the rage and left with a bucket list of things to accomplish in life. Writing a book was on the bucket list.

This book is dedicated to the creator and sustainer of all things. I would be nothing without him.

I am thankful for my parents, Tommie and Jackie. If they didn't hook up, I wouldn't have written this book.

I am thankful for my son, Anthony Thomas. He is my inspiration and joy.

I am thankful for my ancestors. The ones who stayed strong and survived so that I have this opportunity. The only way to repay you is to stay strong, survive, and succeed.

Introduction

I remember the first time I logged onto the internet and saw the World Wide Web. I'd just recently purchased my IBM Aptiva, a cutting-edge machine at the time. A 386 computer with a blazingly fast 56k modem. With internet phone book in hand, Concentric dial-up internet, and Netscape Navigator, I was ready to experience the graphical World Wide Web for the first time.

I dialed in. I heard the dial tones and the all-too-familiar data connection squelch. I was on. Oh, boy! The very first website address I typed in I cannot remember. I do remember the content I saw.

As I sat there and watched a picture download onto my 256-color monitor, I was transfixed. I saw a picture — not saved on my computer or a floppy disk — loading on my screen from who knows where.

The picture that came up on my computer screen was not the reason I was transfixed by it. I was mesmerized by the technology that enabled the picture to appear on the computer screen. I knew at that moment: the internet and World Wide Web were about to become a part of my everyday life.

Little did I know how much so…

One day after that pivotal moment, one of my best friends and I were hanging out. He lamented that he could not find local buyers for the gigantic box of movies he had sitting in the basement of his house. You see, he owned a video store. He had purchased the video cassette inventory (yes, I said video cassettes) of a video store that had gone out of business. His idea was to cherry-pick the videos he needed from the inventory and sell the rest to recoup his investment. Great idea! The challenge he ran up against was that none of the other video stores wanted to purchase new inventory.

After I heard enough bellyaching, I asked him if he knew about the World Wide Web.

"The who?" was his response.

"Never mind," I told him.

Then I asked how much money he needed to get out of each video cassette.

"Five dollars," he said.

I said, "I will tell you what. I'll sell them all for you, and anything over the $5, I keep for myself."

He was skeptical and in a hurry to get his investment money back. He did not have anything to lose. He agreed to the deal.

The next day, I created my first online ad. A classified ad. I placed the ad on a free-use website called www.classified2000.net. Surprisingly, the website is still online after all these years.

Four hours after placing the ad, I received an email in my Hotmail account. "Please send a list."

Uh-oh! Did not think it that far through to make a list! I called my friend.

"I need a list."

"A list for what?"

"A list for all those movies."

"What!?!"

"Yep."

"Damn! Do you remember how many movies are in the basement!?!"

"Yep."

Thirty-six hours later, I had the list. My friend got things done. I learned a lot from him. God rest his young soul.

List in hand and ready to scan (yes, they had scanners back then and OCR), I scanned all the typed pages into a notepad document. I sent the list to my first potential customer from who knows where.

A few hours later, I got a response. The person on the other end of the email, whom I had never met, ordered four video cassettes. Furthermore, he sent his credit card information unsecured and unencrypted. I had access to a merchant account and an online credit card processor, so I was able to run the credit card. Approved.

After a few days, my email inbox was on fire. I got requests for the video list from people I did not know and from places I had never heard of. My operation started to get too big for me to handle. I recruited a friend's wife to help with order fulfillment. She stayed five minutes away from the post office and was online just as much as I was.

I ran the orders over to her around 3:00 p.m. She would package them and ship them when the post office was about to close. It was a sweet deal. She was getting paid. I was getting paid. My friend was recouping his investment. Everybody was happy. I had never experienced anything like it.

One day I got a request for a list, as usual. I sent the list, as usual. The person on the other end of the email replied, "How much for all of the movies?"

I worked out a bulk sales deal with my friend. I sent the asking price to the person on the other end of the email. A few hours later, he responded that he would be up on Saturday at 1:00 p.m. to pick up the movies. This cat lived in Texas.

Now remember that this is 1998, and the commercial World Wide Web was still in its infancy. Online transactions like this happen every day in 2020. Back then, it was rare. I sent him the address of my friend's house. I was skeptical.

I will never forget that day for as long as I live. It was a perfect day. A bright sun, blue sky, not a cloud in sight, 79-degree, fresh-cut grass smell kind of day.

My friend, a couple of other guys, and I were outside in front of his parents' house. We were tossing around the football, playing basketball, and doing stuff that young guys do on a perfect weather day.

Around 1:00, a dark blue, dusty as hell Chevy truck with a trailer pulled into the driveway. The truck stopped, and two guys who definitely looked "Texan" got out of the car "truck" and asked for me. I walked up, shook the guy's hand, and proceeded with the small talk.

After a few minutes, we got down to business. I took him to the movie stash. He went through a good portion of them with his buddy. The guy said that the video cassettes were in great shape. (Most of them were still wrapped in cellophane.) He proceeded to whip out a fat knot of cash, counted out the money, and put it in my hand.

My friend, the other guys, and I helped load the video cassettes into the trailer. We engaged in more small talk; the two Texans got into their truck and drove away. We drove to the party store not too long after they left, bought some drinks, and proceeded to celebrate the most unlikely of business transactions.

I knew then that advertising on the World Wide Web had extraordinary money-making potential. It was at that time that I decided I wanted to be a part of this new world. I acted and never looked back.

Since, I have made over a million dollars for myself and over $18 million for a variety of companies combining the power of smart advertising and the World Wide Web. In this book, I share with you how I achieved this feat. You will learn the principles of smart advertising.

The ideas are presented in the context of over 20 years of experience, mentoring, and study. I believe you will understand how making smart advertising starts with the correct mindset, consequently enabling anyone to sell and make money online using smart words that pay.

Chapter 1

Smart vs. Ignorant Advertising

It is important to understand that there are essentially two types of advertising: smart and ignorant.

Smart advertising forces the consumer to act. It tells the reader, viewer, or listener to do something at the end of the ad. Smart advertising is accountable. When you run smart advertising, you do not run or continue to run ads unless they pay for themselves. You realize as an advertiser that an ad must produce a certain number of sales leads and/or orders for it to be cost-effective. The World Wide Web is hands down the best advertising medium to witness the full power of this idea.

Let me give you an example: Let's say that you've allocated $10 to sell product X. You budget $100 to advertise your product on Google or Facebook. Product X brings back 10 orders for $100. If you budgeted $10 in allowable costs per order to sell your product, then your ad for product X was successful.

On the other hand, let's say that you've spent $100 for an ad which only brought back five orders. Your cost per order was $20. You have doubled your allowable costs to run that particular ad. With smart advertising, the advertiser knows that an ad must yield a certain result.

Ignorant advertising has no call to action. These ads do not ask the viewer to do anything. Therefore, it is hard to measure the profitability or effectiveness of ignorant ads. Ignorant advertising provides reach and visibility. It can also build an image, generate likes and fans, and position a company. All this is great but provides intangible results.

Conversely, all smart advertisers can determine the results of an ad and its profitability. That is the difference between smart and ignorant advertising. Smart advertising must stand on its own and produce a profit.

If you take an ignorant ad and change it to a smart ad, you can immediately measure the results. You will know how many calls, clicks, or visits an ad and a search term or keyword is generating. Why would this help you?

Let me share an advertising anecdote with you. A retailer in New York once said that he knew that 50% of his advertising worked; he just did not know which 50%. By using smart advertising, you will be able to directly track the response and profitability of your ads daily.

People who currently run ignorant ads can save a fortune on advertising by switching to smart ads. Let us say a life insurance company is running a very cute, catchy ad. If that same company switched to advertising a free report or provided valuable information about life insurance in exchange for a call or click, they could begin to get measurable ad results.

Putting Your Ads in the Right Place

Deciding where to place your ads online can be intimidating. Do you advertise on directories? Do you advertise on news media websites? Do you advertise on Google, Bing, or Yahoo? Do you advertise on Facebook, Twitter, Instagram, Snapchat, or other social media websites?

Before you make your decision, you must know who your "perfect customer" is. Male or female? What age bracket? What are their hobbies and interests? Homeowners or renters? Single or married? Answering some of these questions (and more) about who your perfect customer is helps you make smart decisions about where to advertise.

In a nutshell, highly targeted smart advertising will save you time and money. Remember, smart advertising provides you with measurable results; ignorant advertising does not.

Chapter 2

Testing Your Smart Advertising

Most people spend more money than is necessary on initial testing. Online advertising platforms like Facebook Ads or Google Ads will often tell you to spend more money on a test than you need. Why? Google and Facebook make money when you buy ads. Often, they will tell you that you need to spend more money to get more clicks. Yes, this is mostly true, but there is no need to spend big when testing your advertising.

The first thing that we accomplish when we test advertising is determining what kind of messaging inspires your perfect customer to act. We are not looking to make a profit on the first ad; we are just looking to see if anybody acts on the ad messaging. Why would you spend thousands of dollars to determine that when you do not need to?

You should run, at most, two ads against each other (A/B Test) to determine if somebody acts on your advertising message. Usually, two ads will determine response. If it is still questionable, run a couple more ads. Do not ever let an advertising platform "message" you into running large-scale advertising tests. If we run a couple of ads and determine that no one took action, then we either have a problem with your ad, a problem with the product we are offering, or, possibly, a difficulty in placing our ad (right message, wrong audience.)

Let us say that we have run a couple of ads, and we determine that yes, people act on our advertising. What do we do next? We select the ad that got a better response and test that ad against another to achieve the best response rate for our advertising dollar. Example: Let's say that an ad costs you $10, and you get three people to act. Therefore, each response costs you a little over $3. Now we rewrite a new headline for that ad, and we test it against the old ad that we wrote. Our new ad brings back ten responses. That means that we have lowered our response cost by almost 70%! What does that mean? It means that we have dramatically increased our profits.

I have seen one word changed in the headline portion of an ad resulting in a 300% increase in response. When people tell you that advertising headlines or opening statements do not make a difference, do not believe them. They do make a difference, a dramatic difference. As a matter of fact, that is the key to testing your headlines or opening statements. When you change those, you will often see the most dramatic results in your test. Headlines strike a chord with the person reading or viewing your ad. They can ultimately increase the number of responses that you get.

The whole point that I want to get across about testing is this: be patient. If you have an ad that is working, always test against that ad. Try to find an ad that brings better results. If the new ad that you test against your current effective ad brings back 25% better results, all profit falls to the bottom line.

Analyze the results on each ad that you run. The tools available to analyze online advertising results are amazing. Any one of the advertising platforms mentioned earlier has robust measurement tools and can be configured to provide data in various ways and formats.

Test one ad against another; test headlines against each other; test body copy against another; test price; test one guarantee versus another. Continue to test all variables, and you will find that your profits will increase dramatically. Remember: do not spend more money than you need to when you test. Take one step at a time. Be patient; time is on your side with smart advertising.

One of the things that you can do to virtually guarantee profits is to find ads that are already working and try to understand why they are working. Just go online, and pay attention to the ads you see. If you happen to see the same ads repeatedly, it is likely an ad that is working.

Always remember that our first objective in testing is to get someone to raise their hand and say, "I'm interested in your offer." Once we have accomplished that, we can buy more ads.

Chapter 3

How Does Smart Advertising Work?

As I said earlier, smart advertising is accountable. In other words, we know how much each sale or sales lead costs us when we run an ad. How do we discover that? Here is another example: You run an ad at the cost of $100. You have a product that retails for $50. You have budgeted $10 per sale for your online advertising costs. You get 10 responses so your cost to get each order or sales lead is $10. We divide 10 responses into the $100 that we paid for the ad and come up with a $10 cost per order or lead.

Let us say you run that $100 ad, and you get 20 responses. We now have a $5 cost per order. Again, we had a $100 ad, we divided it by 20 responses, and we have a $5 cost per order or lead. On the other hand, let us say we have a $100 ad, and we only get back five responses. We have a $20 cost per order or lead. If our allowable cost to sell our $50 product is $10, and we get a $20 cost per order or lead, what will we do with that ad? We toss it in the trash bin.

Let's look at social media and buying space. Specifically, let's talk about Facebook (I don't advertise on Facebook). A social media website like Facebook does not tell you, "Hey, spend $500 a month for a radio flight or $1,500 on a one-time ad in the newspaper." No. Facebook uses an ad auction format. Rather than showing every ad to everyone, Facebook's ad auction determines which ads to show to create the most value for both the intended audience and the advertiser. That way, people see ads that they are more likely to find interesting and useful, and advertisers reach people who can help them meet their campaign objectives. We know our campaign objectives are always **increased response and return on investment**.

To ensure all ads are evaluated consistently, Facebook assigns a "total value" to every ad that competes in the auction. The total value is based on the amount you bid, how likely it is that showing your ad to a person will lead to your desired outcome, and the quality of the ad — along with how relevant your ad is to the people you want to reach. The ad with the highest total value wins the auction for the people you are trying to reach.

For example, an ad that's very relevant to that person could win the auction, but if another ad with similar relevance to the same person is placed with a higher bid and higher estimated action rates, that ad may win over the first ad.

Let us look at search engines and buying space. Specifically, let's talk about Google. A search engine like Google doesn't tell you, "Yo, throw a few hundred at a radio flight or $5,000 on a one-time ad in the newspaper." No. Google, just like Facebook, uses an ad auction format. Rather than showing every ad to everyone, Google's ad auction determines which ads to show to create the most value for both the intended audience and the advertiser. That way, people see ads that they are more likely to find interesting and useful, and advertisers reach people who can help them meet their campaign objectives. We know our campaign objectives are always **increased response and return on investment**.

Each time a Google ad is eligible to appear for a search, it goes through the ad auction. The auction determines whether the ad shows and in which ad position it will show on the page.

Here is how the auction works:

- When someone searches, the AdWords system finds all ads whose keywords match that search.
- From those ads, the system ignores any that are not eligible such as ads that target a different country or are disapproved.
- Of the remaining ads, only those with a sufficiently high Ad Rank may show. Ad Rank is a combination of your bid, ad quality, and the expected impact of extensions and other ad formats.

The most important thing to remember is that even if your competition bids higher than you do, you can still win a higher position — at a lower price — with highly relevant keywords and ads.

Since the auction process is repeated for every search on Google, each auction can have potentially different results depending on the competition at that moment. Therefore, it is normal for you to see some fluctuation in your ad's position on the page and whether your ad shows at all.

Chapter 4

Headlines

Headlines and opening statements are the most important part of an advertisement. If you do not stop a reader, viewer, or listener right in their tracks with your headline, then you never will. People do not read ads to read them. People read ads because they are interesting. People do not listen to ads to listen to ads. They listen to ads that are interesting. The same goes for viewing ads. People want to know what is in it for them.

What is the best way to use them?

One of the things that I suggest when you are running advertising, is to keep your headlines short. Use three words. Sometimes, one- and two-word headlines will be amazingly effective for you. People try to tell too much in a headline. Do not get me wrong: there are some excellent headlines that are more than three words. But for smart advertising, try to write extraordinarily strong, two- or three-word headlines. They will usually be more effective in getting the attention of your reader. Plus, advertising headlines on Facebook, Google, and so on are limited by the number of characters.

Understand what the headlines do and why they are successful.

Number one: they get attention. Your headline must stop the reader and make them want to read the rest of your ad. You only have one to two seconds to catch someone's attention. In some cases, not only do they get attention, but they create curiosity — curiosity that must be satisfied by reading, listening to, or viewing an ad.

As a bonus gift to you, I will send you the "Essential Headline and Attention Grabber Companion Guide" containing tested and proven headlines. These are some of the most effective headlines ever written. I have done this for a reason. By looking at some of these great headlines, you will discover some that can help you decide how to better advertise your product or service. The included examples that you will read are tested winners.

Using the same headlines and headline formats, but just changing a few words, can make a huge difference in response. You will find that these headlines are tried and true, and they will work for you. Take time to study these headlines. You will find that they get people's attention.

I will also give you certain words that are successfully used in the copy to get people's attention. They reinforce major benefits and major points. These words are difficult for people to pass by. They cause people to stop and listen, view, or read. These words, again, like the headlines, are proven. They evoke emotions in people. Emotions sell. They will help you clearly describe, in action terms, benefits that you can communicate about your product. They serve as information to your prospective customer.

Chapter 5

The Psychology of Advertising That Wins

When you create an ad, the first thing to do is to sit down and ask yourself, "What am I offering to someone who is a potential customer?" If you cannot answer that question, you are certainly not ready to write an ad. As a matter of fact, many ads never answer that question. That is a shortcoming of ignorant advertising. In many cases, there is no message.

Advertising affects four areas of the human brain:

1. Left brain ads are copy-driven ads and have nothing but copy.
2. Right brain ads have nothing but pictures.
3. Whole brain ads combine pictures with copy.
4. No brain ads contain no message whatsoever. They may get attention; they are flashy, and the advertiser's logo is visible, but people have no idea what the advertiser is selling.

One of my early mentors sold a support pillow. He found through testing that more people had pain than suffered from snoring. He reworked his ads and emphasized the pillow's pain-relieving qualities in his advertising because of that information.

If you do not understand what you are offering, you can't expect your prospect to understand. And if your prospect does not understand what you are offering, it is nearly impossible to make a sale.

The next thing that we want to do is determine if our product, information, or service solves a common problem quickly. How does it solve that problem? We want to be able to put that into our own words so that people understand what is in it for them. That is the key to all great advertisements; people must quickly understand what is in them. Often, the solution to the common problem that you are solving can be communicated in your headline.

Do you have competitors? If so, consider their advertisements when you are creating an ad. Are their ads successful? What emotions are they appealing to? Are there things that you can incorporate from their ads into your own without directly copying their ads? Are there selling propositions that they are missing in their ads that you can include in your ad? Look at your competition, shop your competition. See how they sell their product not only how they advertise their product. What is their product price? What guarantees are they making on their product? What ads are they continuing to run more than others? These will help give you clues about how to write a great advertisement for your offer.

The purpose of advertising is to generate sales and make money. Stay focused on that. The only way you will make money is to always emphasize what is in it for the customer. Make sure this idea comes across clearly when you create your advertising.

If you remember only one thing from writing an ad, remember this: everyone wants to know what is in it for them right away, which is why headlines are so important. Understand that your prospect cares nothing about you, your situation, or your product unless it benefits them. Do not try to be cute when you are selling.

Chapter 6

Competitive Advantage

Every business must have a competitive advantage and must be able to tell people what their competitive advantage is. If you do not have a competitive advantage, it is difficult for someone to whom you are proposing your product, information, or services to give you their business over someone else.

What are some of the competitive advantages that people use?

One of the competitive advantages that people use is price. Selling on price alone can be a competitive advantage. This tactic limits profit margins, however.

Another competitive advantage is a guarantee. It is possible that your guarantee is offered for a longer period than your competitors, which reduces purchasing risk. Whatever your competitive advantage, it needs to be clearly stated and firmly planted into your prospect's mind.

Your competitive advantage, aka the unique selling proposition, is extremely important. It sets you apart from your competition. If your product does have a competitive advantage, you need to make sure that your competitive advantage is related to the prospective purchaser as a benefit.

Your competitive advantage can also be benefits that are clearly giving the prospective purchaser the answer to "What's in it for me?" When you are offering your competitive advantage to your prospective purchaser, make sure that you are specific. Do not speak in generalities.

For instance, if your competitive advantage is price, say, "Our price is 10% lower than all competitors." Then justify why it can be 10% lower. If your competitive advantage is a guarantee, state specifically what is different about your guarantee. Is your guarantee twice as long as that of your competitor? Is it three times as long? Is it a better than risk-free guarantee in which you give the consumer something extra even if they decide to return your product? Be specific.

If your product is twice as strong, twice as durable, or lasts twice as long, explain why. Be specific. Make sure consumers walk away understanding the competitive advantage for your product.

If you do not have a competitive advantage for your product, you may have difficulty selling it. You will be competing against other people, and they will be competing against you. Can you make money in this situation? Sure, you can. But it is much easier when you incorporate what your competitive advantage is versus that of your competitors.

State your competitive advantage in terms that are specific or that clearly distinguish why your product, information, or service is unique and better for a prospective customer than anyone else in your field.

Chapter 7

Benefits Versus Features

Understand what the key benefit of your product is. People buy on benefits, not on features. What is the difference? Benefits are things that can help improve the life of the person who is a potential customer for your offer. Features are just things that the product does; they don't have any benefit for your customer.

Let me give you an example. Let us use automobiles. An automobile might have the benefit of going from 60 m.p.h. to 0 in five seconds because it has anti-lock brakes. A feature of the car is interior map lights. The benefit of anti-lock brakes could save your life. Do you see the difference? One is a nicety, and the other makes a difference in a person's life. Think about how many lives have been saved by anti-lock brakes. Think about the emotion that you could build around advertising, emphasizing the life-saving potential of anti-lock brakes. A family's life could be saved in one single second because they spent the extra money or made an educated decision to go with an automobile that offers anti-lock brakes. See the difference? Understand what you are offering.

Benefits help inform our decision to purchase a product. When you look at writing an effective ad, list all the possible benefits that you can offer. Write them down and incorporate them as strategically as possible in your ads. When you are writing an ad, try to incorporate those benefits, and categorize them. Rank those benefits in order of their importance.

Of course, when you run your first ads, you won't know the key benefits unless you follow up with or survey people who purchase your product. Understanding this, you can position ads and play off-key benefits. We may find that what we thought originally were the motivating reasons for people to purchase are not. On the other hand, we may find the benefits that we considered to be of extraordinarily little interest are much more important.

A technique that can be wildly successful is to relay the benefits of your products, information, or services through testimonials: through actual words said by people that are not actors. Testimonials reinforce the value of what ad you are offering. They can relay the benefits of what you are offering to your new prospective purchaser. Testimonials are disarming. People identify with real people.

Testimonials can be received by asking for them via a survey or by emailing your customer base. What did they think about it? Did they enjoy it? What made them purchase the product, and are they glad they purchased it? Ask people if you can use their comments. Get them to sign a release.

Chapter 8

How to Make Offers Irresistible

Have you ever ordered a product that you really did not want, but the bonus to buy was so good that you had to order? Great bonuses will increase the sales of every offer.

What can you offer as a bonus to your product, service, or information? What can help to increase its value? One of the things that I like is products that cost very little but have a high perceived value. **Information is a great bonus to almost any product.**

Back in the day, *Sports Illustrated* magazine offered a free video with Larry Bird, Magic Johnson, or Michael Jordan with the purchase of a subscription. This offer was remarkably successful for one simple reason: They spent more than half of the commercial time selling the free bonus, when, in fact, the real offer was the magazine subscription.

The guarantee that *Sports Illustrated* offered was to keep the video even if you were unhappy with your subscription. You could cancel at any time and get a refund on undelivered magazines. Did a lot of people take them up on their guarantee and cancel their subscription? No. Why did most of the people purchase? For the free bonus offer. It was so good that it was hard to say no.

If people wanted a *Sports Illustrated* magazine subscription, they would have purchased one a long time ago. But this offer was so valuable and interesting that they felt compelled to order. In fact, they were hooked by the bonus. Think about it in your case.

Can you offer something, whether it is information, a video, audio, or another product? Does it complement your product? Can it increase the value of what you are offering? Can you incorporate it into your guarantee so the consumer feels more at ease becoming your customer? Let them know that they can return the product and keep what you have included as a free bonus just because they took the time to review your product, information, or service.

Sit down and think about this whenever you make an offer. How can you take the risk of deciding away from the consumer? How can you make the offer so compelling that it is hard to say no?

People love to get something for nothing. They feel good when they are not at risk. They want to know that they can get their money back and even get something extra just to give it a try. Do this with every product that you offer. Include a bonus along with a guarantee. Do a lot of people take advantage of you? Some will but not that many.

I have consulted with many companies that have discarded this philosophy because they feel that it will not help when, in fact, it will. They are always afraid that someone will take advantage of them. Because they are fearful, they never test; they never see if adding a guarantee and a bonus will increase sales. Those that I have persuaded to use this concept immediately realize sales increases no matter what they were selling.

Go the extra mile and make your offer irresistible by adding valuable bonuses. You can often find very inexpensive bonuses to go along with your product, information, or service. Bonuses make it easier for your prospect to decide. Not only will they know that they can get their money back if they are not happy with what you are offering, but they are getting something extra just for giving it an honest try. This helps change your potential customer's psychology by letting them know that they are not at risk; you are.

Another thing to consider making your offer more appealing is terms. Terms can make it easier for someone to purchase. If you have a $100 product, can you split it into three payments of $33? Most people buy on monthly payments in this country and many countries throughout the world. If you change your offer from a single payment of $100 to three payments of $33, you will typically increase your response by 100%. You have just made it easier for your prospect to purchase. Try to make your terms better than those of your competitors.

It is also important to tell people how easy it is to buy whenever you are running an ad. Most of my ads end with "It's easy to order. All you have to do is..." and then tell the prospect what to do. Walk them through the process step-by-step. Use simple words that are easy for them to understand. Make the process of ordering as easy as possible.

A great example of this type of philosophy in ordering is Amazon.com. Do you know what they do very well? They make it super easy for people to purchase, and they do it in a very disarming way. You can put items in a shopping cart or on a wish list. You can send people a notice that whatever the product is will make a great gift. You can make payments in some cases. You can make purchases with just "one click." And if you are an Amazon Prime member, you can get free 2-day shipping along with a truckload of other "Prime" benefits like video, music, and books. Amazon.com has learned over the years that these approaches make it quite easy for people to act. As a rule, when you ask people to order, the fewer steps they must go through, the better. It makes it easier for them to act on their desires and emotions.

If possible, try to get across to potential customers that it is easy to do business with your company. Let them know that you handle issues quickly, without any hassles, and that you will give them their money back if it comes down to it. Reassure them of this. As I said before, if you can offer a bonus, let them know that they can keep the bonus just because they have taken the time to purchase your product.

You can further increase your orders by letting them know that not only will they get their money back if they decide to return the product and keep their bonus but you will also pay for their shipping and handling.

These techniques, when thoroughly tested, can increase your response.

Correspondingly, your net profits can rise dramatically. Always test these techniques in small scales so that you don't lose money if your test goes wrong. History proves that these concepts work in certain applications and with certain businesses. When you notice effective advertising and great offers, take the time to make a note of those offers. Study them. Understand what makes them great.

I have folders upon folders of great offers I've saved over the years. I have done so because whenever I am stumped, I look back at some of the compelling offers that I've received. I reorganize my thinking and priorities to stay focused on making sure that I can get the best offer possible to the prospective purchaser in my appeal.

Finally, the element that is missing in most ads is urgency. A reason to act now. If you do not have urgency in your ad, then you are leaving the prospect hanging. Give them a reason to act now.

For example, it could be "The first 500 people who respond to this ad get the following bonus" or "The first 100 people to take action will receive this product free for 30 days." No matter what it is, give them a reason to decide now. They will forget if they do not. **Urgency is the key to closing the sale.** If you have a great urgency and you have a terrific offer, you are almost certain to hit a home run in online advertising.

Essential Headline and Attention Grabber Companion

The "Essential Headline and Attention Grabber Companion Guide" contains headlines that are tested and proven. These are some of the most effective headlines ever written.

Also included are high-performing money-making words that are successfully used in copy to get people's attention. They reinforce major benefits and major points. These words are difficult for people to pass by. They cause people to stop and listen, view, or read. These words, again, like the headlines, are proven. Use them.

Greatest Headlines Ever Written

The Secret of Making People Like You

A Little Mistake That Cost a Farmer $3,000 a Year

Advice to Wives Whose Husbands Don't Save Money – By a Wife

The Child Who Won the Hearts of All

Are You Ever Tongue-Tied at a Party?

How a New Discovery Made a Plain Girl Beautiful

How to Win Friends and Influence People

The Last 2 Hours Are the Longest – And Those Are the 2 Hours You Save

Who Else Wants a Screen-Star Figure?

Do You Make These Mistakes in English?

Why Some Foods "Explode" in Your Stomach

Hands That Look Lovelier In 24 Hours – Or Your Money Back

You Can Laugh at Money Worries – If You Follow This Simple Plan

Why Some People Almost Always Make Money in the Stock Market

When Doctors "Feel Rotten" This Is What They Do

It Seems Incredible That You Can Offer These Signed Original Etchings – For Only $5.00 Each

Five Familiar Skin Troubles – Which Do You Want to Overcome?

Which of These $2.50 to $5.00 Best Sellers Do You Want for Only $1.00 Each?

Who Ever Heard of A Woman Losing Weight – And Enjoying 3 Delicious Meals at the Same Time?

How I Improved My Memory in One Evening

Discover the Fortune That Lies Hidden in Your Salary

Doctors Prove 2 Out of 3 Women Can Have More Beautiful Skin in 14 Days

How I Made a Fortune with a "Fool Idea"

How Often Do You Hear Yourself Saying: "No, I Haven't Read It: I've Been Meaning To!"

Thousands Have This Priceless Gift – But Never Discover It!

Whose Fault When Children Disobey?

How a "Fool Stunt" Made Me a Star Salesman

Have You These Symptoms of Nerve Exhaustion?

Guaranteed to Go through Ice, Mud or Snow – Or We Pay the Tow!

Have You a "Worry" Stock?

How a New Kind of Clay Improved My Complexion in 30 Minutes

161 New Ways to a Man's Heart – In This Fascinating Book for

Cooks

Profits That Lie Hidden in Your Farm

Is the Life of a Child Worth $1 to You?

Everywhere Women Are Raving About This Amazing New Shampoo

Do You Do Any of These Ten Embarrassing Things?

Six Types of Investors – Which Group Are You in?

How to Take Out Stains…Use (Product Name) and Follow These Easy Directions

Today…Add $10,000 to Your Estate – For the Price of a New Hat

Does Your Child Ever Embarrass You?

Is Your Home Picture-Poor?

3 Delicious Ways to Give Your Children Extra Iron

To People Who Want to Write – But Can't Get Started

This Almost-Magical Lamp Lights Highway Turns Before You Make Them

The Crimes We Commit Against Our Stomachs

The Man with the "Grasshopper Mind"

They Laughed When I Sat Down at the Piano – But Then I Started to Play!

Throw Away Your Oars!

How to Do Wonders With a Little Land!

Who Else Wants Lighter Cake – In Half the Mixing Time!

Little Leaks That Keep Men Poor

Pierced by 301 Nails…Retains Full Air Pressure

No More Backbreaking Garden Chores for Me – Yet Ours Is Now the Showplace of the Neighborhood

Often a Bridesmaid, Never a Bride

How Much Is "Working Tension" Costing Your Company?

To Men Who Want to Quit Work Someday

How to Plan Your House to Suit Yourself

Buy No Desk – Until You've Seen This Sensation of a Business Show

Call Back These Great Moments at the Opera

I Lost My Bulges – And Saved Money Too

Why (Brand Name) Bulbs Give More Light This Year

Right and Wrong Farming Methods – And Little Pointers That Will Increase Your Profits

New Cake-Improver Gets You Compliments Galore!

Imagine Me – Holding an Audience Spellbound for 30 Minutes

This Is Marie Antoinette – Riding to Her Death

Did You Ever See a "Telegram" from Your Heart?

Now Any Repair Job Can Be "Duck Soup" for You

New Shampoo Leaves Your Hair Smoother – Easier to Manage

It's a Shame for You to Not Make Good Money – When These Men Do It So Easily

You Never Saw Such Letters as Harry and I Got About Our Pears

Thousands Now Play Who Never Thought They Could

Great New Discovery Kills Kitchen Odors Quick! – Makes Indoor Air "Country Fresh"

Take This 1-Minute Test – Of an Amazing New Kind of Shaving Cream

Announcing…The New Edition of the Encyclopedia That Makes It Fun to Learn Things

Again She Orders…"A Chicken Salad, Please"

For the Woman Who Is Older Than She Looks

Where You Can Go in a Good Used Car

Check the Kind of Body You Want

"You Kill That Store – Or It'll Run You Out of the State!"

Here's a Quick Way to Break Up a Cold

There's Another Woman Waiting for Every Man – And She's Too Smart to Have "Morning Mouth"

This Pen "Burps" Before It Drinks – But Never Afterwards

If You Were Given $200,000 to Spend – Isn't This the Kind of (Type of Product, But Not the Brand Name) You Would Build?

"Last Friday…Was I Scared! – My Boss Almost Fired Me!"

67 Reasons Why I Would Have Paid You to Answer Our Ad a Few Months Ago

Suppose This Happened on Your Wedding Day!

Don't Let Athlete's Foot "Lay You Up"

Are They Being Promoted Right Over Your Head?

Are We a Nation of Low-Brows?

A Wonderful Two Year's Trip at Full Pay – But Only Men with Imagination Can Take It

What Everybody Ought to Know…About This Stock and Bond Business

Money-Saving Bargains from America's Oldest Diamond Discount House

Former Barber Earns $8,000 in 4 Months As a Real Estate Specialist

Free Book – Tells You 12 Secrets of Better Lawn Care

Greatest Gold Mine of Easy "Things to Make" Ever Crammed into One Big Book

$80,000 in Prizes! Help Us Find the Name for These New Kitchens Now!

Own Florida Land This Easy Way…$10 Down and $10 a Month

Take Any 3 of These Kitchen Appliances – For Only $8.95 (Values up to $15.45)

Save 20 Cents on 2 Cans off Cranberry Sauce – Limited Offer

One Place-Setting Free for Every Three You Buy!

Using a Lawyer May Be Dangerous to Your Wealth

The People Who Read This Book Will End up with Your Money

The Truth About Getting Rich

Own a Business of Your Choice without Investing 1 Cent

How to Make a Fortune Today Starting from Scratch

The Secret to Being Wealthy

Do Your Employers Work As Slowly As They Read?

Dare to Be Rich

Make Anyone Do Anything You Mentally Command – With Your Mind Alone!

How to Rob Race Tracks Legally

A Startling Fact about Money

How to Discover What You Are Really Good at

No Office – No Phones – No Hassles – Just Cold Hard Cash in the Mail!

The Most Expensive Mistake of Your Life

How to Write a Business Letter

7 Ways to Collect Your Unpaid Bills

How to Start from "Scratch" and Become a PO Box Millionaire

Have You Ever Seen a Grown Man Cry?

Need More Money?

Want to Be a Legal Investigator?

Stop Dreaming and Start Making Money

Fatten Your Bank Account

Investors, Strike Pay Dirt!

How to Write a Good Advertisement

California Lawyer Discovers How to Make Money at Home with the Help of the U.S. Government

How to Burn Off Body Fat Hour-by-Hour!

How the Experts Buy and Sell Gold and Silver

Do You Sincerely Want to Be Rich?

Does Uncle Sam Owe You Money You Don't Even Know About?

The Amazing Lost Money Secret of the U.S. Government

But What If You Could See Her Naked?

The Secret of Having Good Luck

How to Get Rich Reading Classified Ads

How to Form Your Corporation without a Lawyer for Under $50.00

7 Steps to Freedom

How to Write a Hit Song and Sell It

If You Read Nothing Else – Read This

Who's Making a Bundle

Science Has Finally Counterfeited a Perfect Diamond!

Sell Your Product on National Television for a Percentage of Profit

You Don't Know Me, I Realize…But I Want You to Have This Before It's Too Late

Get Out of Debt in 90 Minutes without Borrowing

How to Obtain Guaranteed Credit Anywhere in the United States

The Art of Selling by Telephone

Banking Secrets That Banks Don't Want Published

The Lazy Man's Way to Riches

Attention Grabber Words

Crucial	Survival
Economic Needs	Concept
Envision	Rewards
Security for Your Dollar	Revolution
Obsession Epidemic	Merit
Insatiable	Scorecard
Exercising	Frontier
Forecast	Show Me
Alert	Fueling
Novel	Destiny
Mania	Competitive Edge
Shrewd	Tech Revolution
Remarkable	Dynamics
Enterprising	Renaissance Spirit
Surging	Promising
Reviewing	Buyer's Guide
Gut Feelings	Hybrid

Late-Breaking	Challenging
Value Line	Breakthrough
Monitor	Avoiding
Unlock	Test Drive
Imagination	Block Busting
Masterpiece	Word-of-Mouth
Reminiscent	High Tech
Traces	Views from an Investor
Gaining on	Formula
Lively	Daring
Excitement	Savvy
Whose Time Has Come	Revisited
Under-Priced	Soar
Brave	Compromise
Lively Market	Innovative
Recruiting	Spotlight
Allure	Last Minute
Heritage	Focus
Epidemic	Acquisition-Minded
Slash	Bonanza
Flex	Exploit
Just in Time	Effective
Tax-Resistant	Mainstream
Nostalgic	Launching
Liberated	Comprehensive
Emerging Growth	News Wire

Investor's Round Table	Hot Property
Specialized	School of Thought
Cost Shifting	Timely
Endurance	Growth
Longevity	New
Nest-Egg	Spiral
Energy	Ultimate
Investment Report Card	Skill
Portfolio	Pioneering
Profitable Decision	Dividends
Keep in Touch	Investigative
Distinguished	Perspective
Flourishes	Willpower
Successful Switch	Studying for Stardom
Overrated	Billboard

Quotes from the GOATS

Leo Burnett

Leo Burnett spent 40 years in the advertising industry and operated his own advertising agency. This book is a collection of his ideas and thoughts supported by specific examples of his own creativity. His ad agency developed many well-known advertising campaigns including the Campbell Soup Kids and the Jolly Green Giant for Green Giant canned vegetable products.

On the Importance of Subliminal Suggestion in Advertising

- Advertising is everywhere and should be pleasing to the eye, ear, imagination, and intellect.
- Advertising is the standard-bearer for commerce, trade, and industry.
- Advertising gives products and services faces and identifies them by name.
- Most advertising is rejected conscientiously and accepted subliminally.
- Advertisers must use subliminal suggestion because advertising is listened to but not heard.

On Advertising Philosophy

- All trade is conducted in the human mind. Share of mind is reflected in share of market.
- All ads should present a problem, present a solution, demonstrate the solution, and create an urgency to act.
- Advertisers must develop confidence in a product and maintain a uniformly high standard of quality and service. This will increase share of mind in consumers and, therefore, increase share of market. Share of mind revolves around confidence. The messages must be consistent.

On What Makes a Successful Advertisement

The key to good ad copy is to:

a. pinpoint the consumer benefit,
b. approach the benefit emotionally and
c. logically rationalize it.

An accurately focused emotional appeal transcends cost and all other appeals every time.

Three main considerations in writing good ads:

1. What to put in the ad
2. Where to put the ad
3. How to extend the ad's results at the point of sale

Offer the reader something in terms of one of the two basic laws of human nature:

1. Self-preservation
2. Self-enhancement

Don't tell them how good your goods are; tell them how good your goods make them. Give the reader a reason to buy. Completely satisfy the business consciousness.

Ad copy must be:

1. Provocative
2. Cut to the real interests of the reader
3. Be human and believable

Ads must show facts, problems, objectives, and solutions.

Ads must present aesthetic enjoyment (be visually pleasing).

Graphics must support the main idea, not clutter it.

Advertise in good taste.

Do not give offense to races, religions, or political viewpoints.

Give a clear idea of what you are selling and what the clear benefits are.

Don't be different from the "others" if the "others" are right.

Headlines and subheadings should be brief and specific and tell the story quickly.

Headlines and subheadings should be cheerful and positive.

Headlines should stimulate self-interest and curiosity.

Keep the readers nodding in agreement.

Use frank, sincere, warm words in your ad copy.

Direct the message to an individual in a warm and friendly tone.

Avoid a tone of too great perfection. Keep it believable.

Explain without appearing to explain.

Keep ads accurate and truthful. Avoid overstatements and boasting superlatives.

Do not make a statement that cannot be supported by fact. Be specific.

Ask for the order or action in the advertisement.

Conform to Optical Practices

- Use variation, orderly arrangement, short sentences, and crisp paragraphs.
- Avoid more than four type or size changes in one ad. Avoid ALL CAPS and Italic text.
- A picture of a person using an object is far more effective than a picture of the object alone. Express ideas naturally.

Summary

The key to good ads is to achieve believability. Good ads do not just circulate information. They penetrate the public's minds with desires and beliefs. Any fool can write a bad ad, but it takes a genius to keep his hands off a good one.

A $200 trade paper ad can express the real personality of a brand better than a $30,000 magazine page. A good ad deserves repetition and often performs better the second and third time around than it did the first.

Fairfax M. Cone

Fairfax M. Cone started in the advertising industry as a commercial artist and worked his way up in the advertising field. He worked and trained under other well-known successes in advertising including the revolutionary Albert Lasker, of whom he makes mention in several locations throughout the book.

On Advertising

Advertising is the language of business that is used to tell someone something of importance. It is a means of communication with the purpose of delivering a worthwhile message to a specific audience of one.

Always aim your message to one person. Aim what you have to say to someone who has every reason to be interested. If the message is clear, then everyone else who has any reason to be interested will get it. In trying to write to everyone, the chances are that the writer will reach no one. Advertising should not be designed to be clever. Readers don't read advertising for fun.

The "what" in advertising is important, not necessarily the "how."

The confidence the advertiser has in what he has to sell and the real value of his proposition to the right prospect usually make the difference between success and failure. It also keeps him honest.

Figure out what you want to say and get straight to the point. It's a matter of being as direct and simple as you can. For an ad to be useful, it must be clear.

Ads should have honest promises explained sensibly.

Many more advertisements are spoiled by technique rather than lack of it.

You can't tell a reader what you meant to say. He either gets it in a second or you have failed. In an advertisement, you only have one chance — the first. If you fail, you fail entirely.

One should try to write advertising as one would talk. The closer one comes to it, the better one does. Make your proposition complete. The right proposition can be more valuable than any other aspect of the sell.

Words have work to do. It is not the words themselves; it is the message that the words convey that matters.

A typical want ad is a good illustration of what should be in an advertisement. Many ads are poor because of things they contain rather than things they leave out. Advertising should be thoughtful and honest with no exceptions.

Most products have more than one appeal. The key is to figure out which appeal is the most important to the consumer.

It is not enough that a product shall be a good product. It is necessary also that it shall be a good product for the particular reason and purpose that it was selected.

Change in the direction or tone of voice is one of the most debilitating practices in advertising for it leads to excesses of every kind.

Discontinuing a successful advertisement is foolish.

Plan your advertising to convince the skeptical.

Advertising is often fun to make. But when it comes out funny, it is usually disastrous. Advertising, after all, is not a form of entertainment. It is serious business.

Allegory is rarely recommended in advertising except in a few rare instances.

Nothing in television advertisement works like a demonstration — provided that it is dramatic and convincing.

Advertising is a competition that one enters to win.

Three (3) Questions You Need to Answer Before Writing an Advertisement:

1. What is it you are trying to say?
2. What is it you are trying to sell?
3. What is your proposition?

Five Rules of Advertising:

1. Must immediately make clear what the basic proposition is.
2. What is clear must also be important and express a well-defined value.
3. Must express the value of the offering in personal terms. It will be beamed directly at the most logical prospects for the proposition. No one else matters.
4. Good advertising will always express the personality of the advertiser, for a promise is only as good as its maker.
5. A good advertisement will always demand action. It will "ask for the order," so to speak, or it will exact a mental pledge because its promise is not to be denied.

Good Advertising Qualities:

- Advertising should command attention but never be offensive.
- Advertising should be reasonable but never dull.
- Advertising should be original but never self-conscious.
- Advertising should be imaginative but never misleading.

Philosophies

The best way to move people is reasonably.

Don't underestimate someone's intelligence. But don't overestimate their knowledge.

To be right is not sufficient. You must appear right too.

You can't sell a bad product twice to the same person.

Summary

Fairfax M. Cone's successes and failures have been compiled from decades of personal experience and include many famous products and brand names that are easily recognizable.

Claude C. Hopkins

Claude Hopkins spent over 35 years in advertising, and his name is identified with the introduction of coupons used in advertising.

He believes a man who has made a success wants to see others achieve the same, just as one who works wants to see others work in order to reach their goals. He tells us that he learned industry from his mother and poverty from his father.

Both of these lessons helped him to become successful because he applied them to his life and business all of his life. He was always called in to handle emergencies in his work and found each crisis a great challenge.

Some of his more famous advertising was for the VanCamp Pork and Beans Company, Palmolive Soap, and the Quaker Oats Company.

On Advertising Guidelines

A good article is its own best salesman (use samples and coupons).

Relate to the common people (study them and use simple words in short sentences).

Use demonstrations for clarification (better sales).

Make tests, feel out the public pulse. Submit all things to the court of public opinion.

Hopkins advises that the road to success lies through the ordinary people, the vast majority. Good advertising is ordinary. If you understand human nature, you will be successful. Be humble, canny, thrifty, economical, suspicious, and honest.

On Principles of Advertising

Tell the truth in advertising.

Sell service; be altruistic. Please the people.

Pique curiosity.

Offer the privilege of buying.

Create sensation, present enticing ideas, and offer inducements that lead the public to buy.

Use dramatic demonstrations, arouse enthusiasm.

Keep your name before the people.

Don't seek favor or profit for yourself.

Give free samples (try without risk).

In advertising, one must out-bid all others in some way; offer advantages in quality, service, or terms, or create a seeming advantage by citing facts others don't.

You must know your competition and what they offer; know what people want. Hopkins tells us not to underestimate the intelligence and information of people who count their pennies; they are the majority, and they are the ones who buy the products.

On Points Well-Taken

Advertise to the individual, not the masses.

Urge people to try the competitive brand for comparison (be certain of your brand; show confidence).

Don't boast or be selfish; talk service.

Offer an advantage to do business with you.

Tell the facts; a story about your product.

Keep it simple and honest; create the demand.

Inject some personality into your ad campaign.

On Good Advertising

Be specific; state actual figures and facts.

Follow the trend of the crowd and focus on it.

Stay with a certain method that's profitable.

Don't take attention from the subject with stylish writing.

Offer super service.

Arouse interest in the product.

On Lessons Learned

Human nature is the same everywhere.

If you sell the customers, the dealers will supply.

Quick volume is more profitable than slowly developed volume — attain maximum as soon as you can.

Success depends on pleasing people (research will tell you if it's working).

Sell the product, not yourself.

Don't show off.

Offer service.

Don't boast.

Aim to get action (use coupons).

Induce prompt action.

Don't waste space.

Ads should tell the full story.

Tell the truth.

Never advertise negatively.

Summary

Hopkins credits a lot of his success to house-to-house canvassing in earlier years. As a result, his knowledge of human nature helped him to relate to the common man and to believe in the importance of research. He advises us never to judge humanity by ourselves and never to judge by personal preferences or opinion. To be successful, he suggests that an advertising person should study salesmen and canvassers, and he believes that real salesmanship has no regard for price.

Maxwell Sackheim

Maxwell Sackheim started out as an errand boy for a newspaper and went on in mail order/response advertising to create such works as the original "Book and Record Club" advertising for Columbia House and several major literary guilds.

He developed the concepts used today by book and record clubs that include the "of the Month Automatic Shipment Plan" techniques.

On Advertising

Advertising that is admired by advertisers is usually ignored by the consumer.

Testing takes the big gamble out of mail order.

Mail order experience and good business judgment are much more vital to the success of a mail business than is the product experience, ample capital, or any other factor.

Products that are widely available can be successful in mail order—sometimes more so than a product not available anywhere else.

An ad should always be warmly received, believed, and acted upon.

Sell the results of a product rather than the product itself.

Allowing a discount on a first order can eliminate a lot of sales resistance and produce good leads.

Tell if you want to sell.

Human interest makes good ads.

A two-colored ad can actually be less effective than the same ad in black and white. Offering a bargain price for a product or sample can actually be more effective than offering it for free. It is better to offer a good premium at a self-liquidating price than an insignificant premium for free.

All the elements intended to increase the use or utilization of a product contribute to the general prosperity of the product.

An ad should always require an action from the consumer.

Take nothing for granted in an ad — describe every detail.

Always ask these questions of your ads:

1. Why should anyone read it?
2. Why should anyone believe it?
3. Why should anyone do anything about it?

If you can give yourself an acceptable answer to these questions, the ad is probably good.

On Headlines

The headline does the trick. If the headline produces a "So what?" reaction, it is no good. If the reader asks "Where, what, why, who, when, or how," it is probably good. The headline must induce reading of the ad. Some of the strongest words to use in headlines are "free," "new," "stop," "at last," and "don't." A headline that is a question is generally better than a statement. The headline should make a promise. There are always exceptions to these guidelines.

On Symptoms and Cures Advertising

Symptom and cure advertising presents a set of symptoms and then a cure. Find all the symptoms your product can cure. The more universal the symptoms, the wider the market; the more serious the symptom, the more important the cure.

On Sampling a Product

Anything that is light enough to mail, inexpensive enough to distribute widely that requires sight, smell, touch, or taste to be appreciated is worth sampling through advertising.

On Advertising Principles and Techniques

The Four (4) Basic Principles of Advertising:

1. Attract attention
2. Stimulate interest
3. Carry conviction
4. Induce action

Response Advertising

Speeds up distribution.

Introduces products more quickly to the consumer.

Provides salesmen with pre-qualified leads.

Buys customers instead of making impressions.

Stimulates dealer and jobber cooperation.

Enables an advertiser to do several times the amount of advertising he now does for the same amount of money.

The Seven Deadly Advertising Mistakes

1. Give the reader a reason for not reading your ad.

A reader must have an incentive to read the ad. The base of the ad is news. An ad must make a promise.

2. Use headlines that whisper "sweet nothings."

   An ad must arouse an interest in the reader. The headline can make all the difference in the success of an ad. The headline must make the reader want to read more.

3. Use pictures that do not talk.

   Ten words can be worth 1,000 pictures if they are the right words and the wrong pictures. Unless pictures are self-explanatory or give meaning to words, they shouldn't be used. It is better to use no pictures than to use the wrong one.

4. The curse of cleverness.

   Plays on words and clever sayings are rarely a plus in advertising.

5. Go around Robin Hood's barn.

   If the ad requires too many charts, diagrams, and thought processes, it is wrong. The round-about approach seldom gets the sale.

6. Leave 'em dangling.

   Make an offer and give the reader a chance to do something immediately in every ad. An ad must urge action now without allowing time for the reader to forget.

7. Use yackety-yack Copy.

   Don't underestimate the discrimination of the public. The copy must be believable. Don't pat yourself on the back. Don't talk for the sake of hearing your own voice. When words clutter, cut them out. Don't use filler copy.

The Seven Deadly Direct (e)Mail Mistakes

1. Give the prospect a good reason for not opening your mail. This is

accomplished by:

   a. Telling so much on the envelope (so much in the subject line) that the reader knows he does not want what you are offering inside.

   b. Being so smart, clever, or unbelievable as a result of what you print on the envelope (write in the subject line) that the reader says, "no way" or "bullshit" or "more junk mail."

   c. If ad copy is going to be used on the envelope (in the subject line), it should be a strong headline and include news, a promise of information, or an advantage to the reader.

2. Give the reader a reason for not reading your mailing.

   The advertisement must promise the reader an adequate reward for his time and attention. The promise must be for news on what interests him and/or a cure for whatever symptoms he suffers from or can be made to suffer from.

3. Make trivial tests.

4. Testing is a good thing only if there isn't too much of it. There can be a big difference between the result of a test and the result of a mailing. Tests do not always tell the whole truth.

5. Make sales. Not customers.

   Make offers your prospects cannot resist. It is important to make customers so you can get repeat business. Spend more time and thought on ex-customers. Study them and try to get them back.

6. People won't read long letters (emails).

   What is a long letter (email)? Any letter (email) that is uninteresting is a long letter (email). A short letter (email) can seem long, and a long letter (email) can seem short. It is not how you say it; it's what you say. Do not be afraid to use space to tell your story. It is better to tell a good story rather than tell no story.

7. Let the list go to the last.

    Direct mail (email) depends on your ability to select your prospects and aim a "bullet" with your story. One reason many direct mailings (emails) fail is that they are directed at too many wrong people.

    Start with your own list and keep it clear. After that, use lists of mail (email) order buyers of similar products and then mail (email) order buyers of other products who have purchased through a plan similar to yours. Finally, compile lists by occupation or classifications that suit your product. Consult a list broker if needed. Good lists are very important to direct mail (email).

8. Forget that your letters are you.

    Remember that each letter you send is you. Put yourself in as the recipient of the letter. Write to yourself. Each letter is a reflection of you. Be yourself.

Summary

Maxwell Sackheim talks a lot about direct mail given the context of the time when he was alive. The principles are timeless and can be applied to direct email and direct messages.

Vic Schwab

Advertising Age called him "the greatest mail-order copywriter of all time." His contributions to mail order ads, especially for the Dale Carnegie book, "How to Win Friends and Influence People," got Schwab into copywriting. From there he became a research pioneer by using coded coupon ads to split test headlines, appeals, copy length, layouts, and calls to action.

The Five Fundamentals of Writing a Good Advertisement:

1. Get attention.

2. Show people an advantage.
3. Prove it.
4. Persuade people to grasp that advantage.
5. Ask for action.

On Headlines

The primary purpose of a headline is to induce people to start reading the copy of the ad. The copy must get read if the ad is going to win.

The headline must get immediate attention...it must offer a reward for reading...and select the readers interested in that subject.

There are two types of headlines that promise desirable rewards for reading. One does it through a positive approach, the other through a negative one. Here is how they do it:

1. By managing to convey, in a few words, how the reader can save, gain, or accomplish something through the use of your product — how it will increase this: his mental, physical, financial, social, emotional, or spiritual stimulation, satisfaction, well-being, or security.
2. Or, negatively, by pointing out how the reader can avoid (reduce or eliminate) risks, worries, losses, mistakes, embarrassment, drudgery, or some other undesirable condition through the use of your product — how it will decrease this: his fear of poverty, illness, or accident, discomfort, boredom, and the loss of business or social prestige or advancement. Interrogative headlines are also good. They ask a question to which people want to read the answer.

Good headlines contain specific words or phrases that make the ad promise to tell you: how, here's, these, which, which of these, who, who else, where, when, what, why.

Colloquialisms get attention because they sound human and natural.

Using the "which of these" selling technique is very effective because it says, "Which do you want?" and "Do you want?"

Another good headline technique is to play up a powerful guarantee if you, indeed, have one.

Your primary viewpoint should be a "point of you." In other words, talk about the prospect by using words such as you, your, and yourself.

Try to get your reader involved in your ad. Use phrases such as "Take this test." Its purpose is to induce the reader to participate in a demonstration of the product's merits.

Announcement headlines are very effective. People are always interested in new things.

On the Impact of Good Layout

Your ad layout should be one of two things: so powerful that it captures the eye or so uncommonly simple and sedate that it looks nonprofessional and non-threatening.

Your ad should be interesting to look at while conveying the feeling of movement and action. Believe it or not, a little bit of irregularity or disharmony in the design attracts attention.

The use of pictures also increases the attention value. For instance, people like seeing pictures of other people. In order of preference, readers like to see:

1. Photographs of children
2. Groups of adults
3. Sports scenes
4. Animals
5. Natural scenery

When you can, show the product in use. Any illustrations related to the product should do a specific selling job, substantiating and advancing the copy story.

On Showing People Advantages

The thing people want to know above everything else is: WHAT WILL YOUR PRODUCT DO FOR ME? To make your copy hold the attention that your layout and headline have already won, show people an advantage — and keep showing them. Not what the product is, but what it will do for the customer.

Also helpful is to tell the prospect what others will say of him, think of him, do for him; how they will admire him, envy him, imitate him; because of what your product will accomplish for him.

People are more likely to agree with you if you first agree with them by showing them that you have a sympathetic understanding of how they already feel.

On the General Trends of Our Times

Success instead of integrity

Restlessness instead of rest

Desire for new instead of affection for oldSpending instead of saving

Show instead of solidity

Ostentation instead of restraint

Self-Indulgence instead of self-discipline

Dependence instead of self-reliance

Gregariousness instead of solitude

Easy

Generosity instead of wise giving

Luxury instead of simplicity

Quick impressions instead of careful thought

On the Importance of the First Paragraph

The first paragraph of an ad should:

- Follow through with the idea or appeal expressed in the main headline — which is what attracted the reader in the first place.
- Be short, with quick, easy-to-read sentences.
- Perhaps start with a question: one so pertinent or challenging as to grip the reader's interest at once and impel him to keep reading to find the answer.
- Start immediately to carry out the reward-for-reading promise made in the headline.

On Appealing to the Emotions

The way to show people an advantage of your product is to stress appeals to the emotions and instincts for they are the primary motivating forces.

On the Proper Use of Facts

You need facts (proof) in order to create and justify convictions, and you need conviction in order to create and justify sales.

The more facts you present, the more credible your advertisement. Facts will provide the reader with an excuse for buying.

Good copy involves digging for facts before a word is written. A careful search for facts can bring to the surface unsuspected or unexploited angles along with superiorities and advantages of your product.

In presenting facts, start where the reader is. Find some common meeting ground. Get your reader's agreement with familiar facts, and then you can more easily carry him on from the known to the unknown. The use of familiar facts helps to create belief.

When you present facts to prove your case, follow these guidelines:

1. Use statements that sound true, otherwise, they won't be believed.
2. Make your facts specific such as "48.5%" instead of "almost 50%."
3. Use actual photographs rather than drawings.
4. Use facts that will show why the promise can be kept.

On Persuading Your Prospects

The clincher copy may, in a shorter advertisement, represent only one or two sentences. In longer copy, it may represent several paragraphs. But in either case, it is a final setting of the stage preparatory to asking for some specific action on the part of the reader.

It gathers up various threads of claims and proof and weaves them into a strong close. It reiterates. It reminds. It sums up.

"The approach can be negative or positive, but it must have emotion."

"Aim at your hardest target — the people who are the hardest to sell."

On Closing the Sale

Delay is the enemy of a sale so remove any obstacles that stand in front of action on the part of the prospect.

Here are some specific ways to ask for immediate action:

Make an Offer

A booklet, a sample, a free demonstration, an extra premium, an introductory price, a miniature model, a contest, a chart, a free fitting, entry in a contest, special phone rates for ordering, special bonuses for ordering by phone, or other motivating inducements.

Time Limit

Only if such a time limit is bona fide.

Limited Supply

If such is the case, point this fact out forcefully.

Price Going Up

Give a specific date if possible.

Low Price

If you're offering a reduced price, emphasize the benefit of taking advantage of it at once.

Gain or Loss

Stress again what he gains by buying immediately or loses by delaying.

John Caples

John Caples is known for revealing time-tested techniques for increasing the response and the cost-effectiveness of direct response advertising.

Here are seven items that Caples discussed in length that are important for all print advertisers to adhere to:

1. You must test all variables in an ad to get to the maximum sales per dollar.
2. What you say in your ad is more important than how you say it.
3. The headline is, above all, the most important part of your ad.
4. The best headlines that make the most money appeal to the reader's self- interest or give news.
5. Long headlines that say something are better than short headlines that say nothing.
6. Specifics are easier to believe than general statements.
7. Long copy will usually sell more of whatever you're selling than short copy.

Caples divides advertisers into two classes. The first are people who are always testing their ads to get the best results and the most return for their dollar; the second are people who do little or no testing or measuring of the advertising results.

There's Only One Reason Why You Should Advertise: To Get Sales

One advertisement's appeal can out-produce another by as much as 19-1/2 times.

Every ad should use a tracking device such as an extension number or special telephone number if you're asking purchasers to call or a department number if you're asking people to send money through the mail.

By using this method, you can determine how well one ad performs versus another; then you can determine how much that ad costs you to make each sale.

Spend the majority of your time writing an ad on the headline. That's the most important part of your ads.

It's easy to write your copy if you really have a "stopper" of a headline.

Offer the Reader of Your Ad Something They Want

Headlines should arouse the reader's curiosity and appeal to their self-interest.

Try to incorporate self-interest, news, curiosity, and quick, easy solutions to the reader's problems in your ads.

Five Rules for Writing Headlines:

1. Try to get self-interest into your headlines.
2. Try to get news into your headlines.
3. Avoid headlines that just make the reader curious.
4. Avoid headlines that are negative or gloomy. Positive headlines will pour more readers.
5. Try to focus on quick and easy solutions to the reader's problems in your headline.

Different Ways to Write a Headline

1. Use the word "announcing" at the beginning of your headline.
2. Try to use words that have an announcement quality.
3. Use "new" to start a headline.
4. Use "now" to start a headline.
5. Use the phrase "at last" to start a headline.
6. Use a date in your headline.
7. Use a new style when you write headlines.
8. Try to get the price in the headline.
9. Use a reduced price in the headline.
10. Try to incorporate a special offer.
11. Use easy-payment plans.
12. Use free offers.
13. Offer valuable information.
14. Tell a story.
15. Start headlines with: "how to," "how," "why," "which," "who else," "wanted," "this," "advice."
16. Use testimonial-style headlines.
17. Offer the reader a "take this test" headline.
18. Use two-word headlines.
19. Warn the reader about putting the response to the offer off; give them a reason to act now.
20. Address your headlines to a specific group.
21. Let the manufacturer speak directly to the prospect in your headline.

How to Get More Response from Your Ads

Put the offer in the headline, sub-headline, or first paragraph.

Put a lot of emphasis on the word "free."

Show a picture of the product that you're offering.

Use testimonials; include coupons, business-reply postcards, business-reply envelopes, or any device that makes it easy for people to respond.

Test your offers, test your ads, and test the places where you run your ads.

Ask people to act now and give them a reason, or incentive, to do so.

Include a telephone number in your ad.

Study what your competitors are doing.

Keep records of your results.

The Advantage of Using Small Ads

You can run a lot of small ads for the price of one big ad.

Lots of small ads with the right offer can convert prospective clients into actual customers inexpensively.

You can get special positioning and take advantage of the attention that a large ad will get.

What's Next?

Hey, you read the whole thing! Well done!

Now that you have a rock-solid foundation, how do you start using the information to begin selling and making money? Just start.

Find or create a product. Start writing and testing ads.

Send me an email smartads@antblair.com for fee based help or accountability.